Guatemalan Chicken Buses

The Beautiful Afterlives of American School Buses

DANIEL RADIN

Copyright © 2011 Daniel Radin

All rights reserved.

ISBN: 1460986962
ISBN-13: 978-1460986967

DEDICATION

Dedicated to Eliza Strode who introduced me to Guatemala and all of its beauties.

CONTENTS

Acknowledgments	i	Gonzalez	22
Introduction	1	Irma	24
Aleja Nora	2	Lilian	26
Antonieta	3	Maria Jose	27
Belmont	6	Mi Linda Floricita	28
Brendita	8	Norma	29
Brisas	9	Primorosa	31
California	11	Princesita	33
Camelia	12	Red Yellow	35
Charro	13	Samantha	37
Dorita	14	Santa Fe 1	38
Esmeralda	15	Santa Fe 2	42
Gabriela	20	Vasquez	45
		Yolanda	46

ACKNOWLEDGMENTS

I would like to thank all of the drivers, mechanics, and artists who created these beautiful and useful sculptures on wheels.

INTRODUCTION

When American school buses reach the age of ten years or 150,000 miles, they are sold at auction. Many of these buses are bought and driven down through Mexico to Guatemala where they are prepared for their second lives. In contrast to their modest first lives as yellow buses carting children to school, their second lives are spent stuffed with people, topped with roof racks full of cargo, and driving at high speeds over mountain passes. The old yellow paint is covered with colorful murals and praises to Jesus. This book is a tribute to those second lives and to the people who share them with these "chicken buses."

The name that starts each section is the name of the bus company, not the bus itself. I generally chose one style of bus from each company. The only exception was Santa Fe. I was so in love with their buses that I had to include two styles. The "Red Yellow" bus was not labeled with a name so I just labeled that section with the color combination.

ALEJA NORA

They must add fresh ribbons every day. Note the hood ornament and the fancy antennas. They also added extra fog lights on the side mirrors.

ANTONIETA

The buses all compete for the same passengers. A shiny clean bus tells customers that it is well maintained and safe.

The driver's helper makes sure all of the chrome is bright and shiny.

Satisfied with his work, he heads back on the bus.

BELMONT

What a beauty! Note all of the custom decals on the big chrome bumper. Especially the sexy girls!

Here's another one of their buses loading up and getting ready to go. Note the cargo on the roof.

BRENDITA

Smurf, Snoopy, and of course, the sexy girl!

BRISAS

This one has beautiful red, white, and blue detail work. It also sports the Bluebird logo. Bluebird is the American company that makes the most desirable school bus bodies.

Note the table and the basket on the roof. The green buckets are for washing the bus. And of course, every bus needs to carry a spare tire. There is no roadside service available.

CALIFORNIA

Here is another one with the Bluebird logo.

CAMELIA

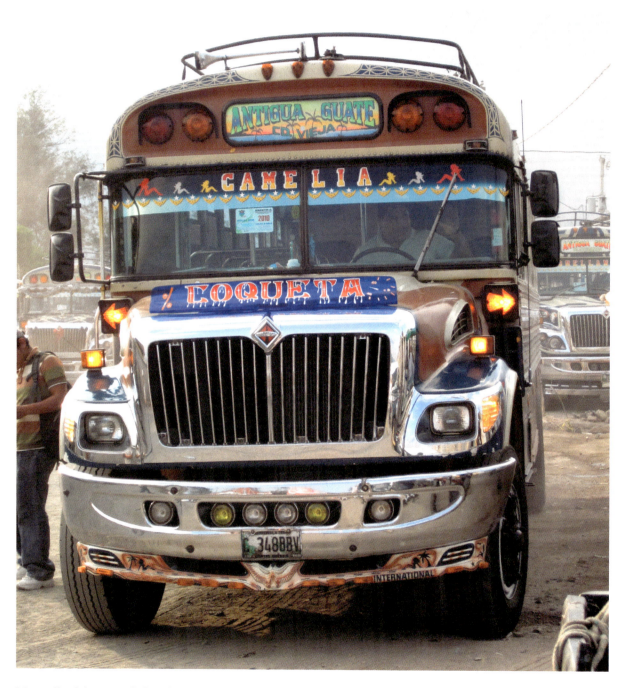

Note all of the extra lights that are necessary for the places these buses go.

CHARRO

I love the eagle head and wing on the side of the hood. Even the destination sign is written in a great stylized typeface.

DORITA

Big bold front grills are a common addition, as are the painted pieces under the front bumpers.

ESMERALDA

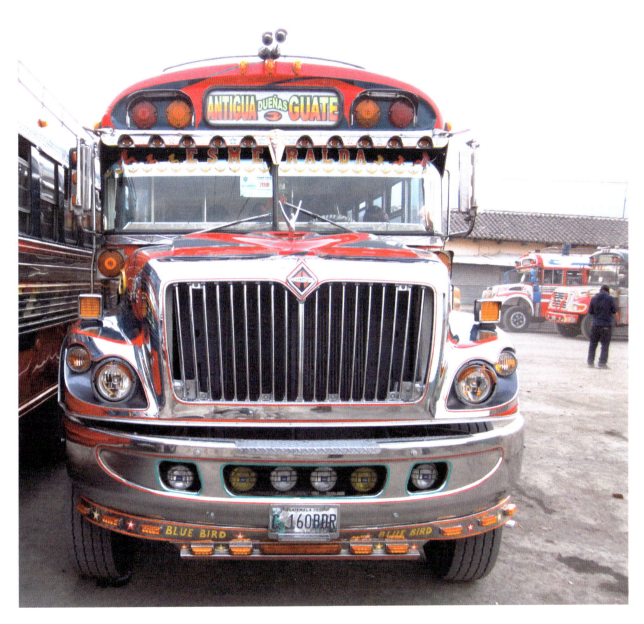

This bus has it all! Note the treatment above the windshield.

It's a work of art!

I love the swan hood ornament. It is not uncommon to see proud references to the American origins of these buses.

Is that Yosemite Sam on the mud flap? Even the wheel-balancing weights are decorated with bright yellow paint. Only in Guatemala! This is obviously a company that takes great pride in their product.

The black chrome back window tint goes perfectly with the color scheme. And you have to love the lion!

GABRIELA

Check out the Road Runner!

What's this guy's name?

GONZALEZ

Here are some happy children coming from the bus.

The driver takes a break.

IRMA

This one is covered with decorations including another Road Runner.

"This bus is protected by the blood of Jesus. The key is in heaven."

LILIAN

It's amazing to think that these are the same buses that once took American kids to school. They remind me more of American muscle cars.

MARIA JOSE

Each bus has a crew of two, the driver and his assistant. The assistant often runs ahead drumming up business. He is also responsible for securing the cargo on the roof and collecting fares.

MI LINDA FLORICITA

This one still looks like a school bus. The horse on the front is a nice touch though.

NORMA

Jesus watches over the sexy girl.

PRIMOROSA

Once again, we see a nice use of custom tinting on the back window.

PRINCESITA

This bus is proud of its American roots. I love the way the artist accentuates the shape of the headlight frame.

RED YELLOW

I don't know that name of the company, but I love the paint job! Note the custom hood scoop and chrome windshield overhang.

What is he doing up there?

SAMANTHA

It looks like bicycles up front and weavings in the back. There are also lots of fun decorations on the windows. And check out those windshield wipers!

SANTA FE 1

This was probably my favorite bus!

That grill is unreal!

I just couldn't get enough of it!

Every detail is a work of art!

SANTA FE 2

Here's another beauty from the Santa Fe company.

VASQUEZ

This one still looks very much like a school bus but I love the flames.

YOLANDA

This one has some nice color choices. This is a typical position of the driver's assistant.

That's the end of my photo essay from sunny Guatemala!

Made in the USA
Charleston, SC
03 January 2013